Frederick George Lee

Lyrics of Light and Life

Frederick George Lee

Lyrics of Light and Life

ISBN/EAN: 9783744796385

Printed in Europe, USA, Canada, Australia, Japan

Cover: Foto ©Thomas Meinert / pixelio.de

More available books at **www.hansebooks.com**

LYRICS OF LIGHT AND LIFE.

Lyrics of Light and Life:

LIV. *Original Poems by*

Dr. JOHN H. NEWMAN, William Alexander, Bp. *of* Derry, Christina G. Rossetti, Aubrey de Vere, J. C. Earle, W. Chatterton Dix, Rev. Gerard Moultrie, Rev. Henry Nutcombe Oxenham, Rev. R. H. Baynes, H. W. Mozley, Rev. A. M. Morgan, Rev. Edward Caswall, B. Montgomerie Ranking, Rev. R. S. Hawker, Rev. John Purchas, Rev. W. J. Blew, Rev. Dr. Monsell, Hedley Vicars, H. M. Stuart, D. Mackworth Dolben, &c. Edited by the Rev. Frederick George Lee, D.C.L.

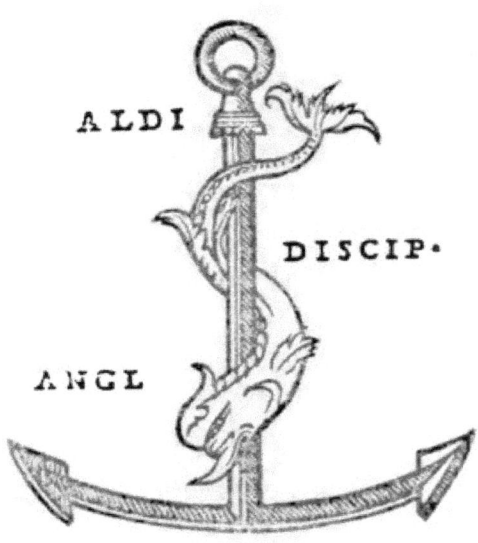

LONDON: PICKERING & CO., 196, PICCADILLY.

1878.

Second Edition, Revised and Enlarged.

Forte scutum Salus Ducum.

Dedicated with Respect and Regard to the Right Honourable Thomas Fortescue, Lord Clermont,

 FIDE ET  CONSTANTIA.

And to Louisa, Lady Clermont, of Ravensdale Park, in the County of Louth.

✠ *Beati*  *pacifici.*

PREFATORY NOTE.

I CANNOT send forth this volume without placing on record my great obligations, and heartiest thanks, to all those whose valued and truly-prized contributions have made it what it is. This I now do.

Planned more than ten years ago, and put aside for some time by other and more pressing duties, it has been to me at once an agreeable relaxation and a very great pleasure, from time to time, to secure from many friends and others the various Christian Lyrics which follow,—for which I here express my sincere acknowledgments. I feel deeply honoured by having been permitted to gather and arrange such a poetical posy; and this from so many who have won their laurels.

Two of the contributors, whose memories are frequently before me, my old and dear friend the Rev. John Purchas, and Mr. Mackworth Dolben, of Finedon Hall,—a young writer of intense refinement, deep spirituality, and great promise, (who met an untimely death,) have passed away from sight and ken.

The poems of these writers may be all the more valued, therefore, because with them the pen has been laid down, the hand is cold, and the heart is still.

I have only to add that no author is responsible for anything more than his own contribution.

F. G. L.

All Saints' Vicarage, Lambeth,
November 4, 1874.

NOTE TO THE SECOND EDITION.

IT is a source of satisfaction to me that a book which appealed neither to the ordinary multitude nor to commonplace tastes, has so soon reached a second edition. This, having been carefully revised, only differs from the first in that it contains eleven new poems. To the respective authors of these I tender my sincere acknowledgments.

Since its publication three more of the original contributors have passed onward to the life beyond the grave—Mr. Hawker, the Vicar of Morwenstow; Father Caswall, of the Birmingham Oratory, and Dr. Monsell. *Requiescant in pace.*

F. G. L.

Invention of the Holy Cross,
1878.

TABLE OF CONTENTS.

	AUTHOR.	PAGE
Below and Above	Lord Bishop of Derry	1
My Birthday	Very Rev. J. H. Newman, D.D.	6
A Rose Plant in Jericho	Miss Christina G. Rossetti	11
The Silver Army	Rev. John Purchas, M.A.	13
The Basilica of St. Mark, Venice	Rev. F. G. Lee, D.C.L.	18
A May Carol	Aubrey de Vere, Esq.	20
From the Cloister	Digby Mackworth Dolben, Esq.	22
Desecration	W. Chatterton Dix, Esq.	28
On the Baptism of a Child	Miss Nora Batt	31
The Death of Ermengarde	Aubrey de Vere, Esq.	35
India's Dream	Rev. Arthur Middlemore Morgan, M.A.	37
Our Rest	Mrs. Frederick George Lee	41
The Sister of Mercy	Folliott Sandford Pierpoint, Esq.	44
The Other Side	Rev. R. H. Canon Baynes, M.A.	54
White is the colour of Angels	Rev. George Akers, M.A.	56
Our Lady of the Snows	"B."	59

Contents

	AUTHOR.	PAGE
"Let the Hills hear Thy Voice"	Rev. Henry Nutcombe Oxenham, M.A.	62
The Servant of Christ	Rev. J. S. B. Monsell, LL.D.	66
Golden Rays	C. A. M. W.	69
Dreams	Rev. John Purchas, M.A.	72
In Hoc Signo Vince	Anonymous	73
Angelus Domini	Digby Mackworth Dolben, Esq.	76
The Child's Offering	Rev. William Edward Green, M.A.	79
A Dream of Paradise	Miss Helen Montagu Stuart	84
The Bread of Life	Anonymous	87
River Thoughts	Rev. W. J. Blew, M.A.	91
Purbrook, Hampshire	Rev. Arthur M. Morgan, M.A.	94
Hymn after Holy Communion	Anonymous	96
Salve mi Angelice	H. W. Mozley, Esq., M.A.	98
A Legend of the Weeping Willow	B. Montgomerie Ranking, Esq.	102
The Holy Souls	Mrs. Frederick George Lee	104
The Trouvère	Aubrey de Vere, Esq.	107
Hymn of Praise	Rev. J. S. B. Monsell, LL.D.	108
The Ship in the Storm	"Y. N."	111
Corporate Reunion	John Charles Earle, Esq., B.A.	114
Super Flumina	Folliott Sandford Pierpoint, Esq.	115
Immaculata	Aubrey de Vere, Esq.	118
Another fleeting Day is gone	"I."	121

Contents. xi

	AUTHOR.	PAGE
In God's Sight	Rev. Edward Cajwall, M.A.	122
Thy Kingdom Come. No. I.	Rev. William Edward Green, M.A.	124
Thy Kingdom Come. No. II.	Rev. F. G. Lee, D.C.L.	126
The Two Crowns	Folliott Sandford Pierpoint, Esq.	131
Eventide	Hedley Vicars	134
Hymn for All Saints' Day	Rev. Gerard Moultrie, M.A.	136
The Great Cloud of Witnesses	Authoress of "The Departed and other Verses"	138
Unknown Graves	Rev. F. G. Lee, D.C.L.	141
Manet Sabbatismus	B. Montgomerie Ranking, Esq.	144
Compline Hymn	Anonymous	147
Light in the Darkness	Norval Clyne, Esq.	149
For a Young Girl with a Book of Carols	Rev. W. J. Blew, M.A.	153
Rest	Anonymous	155
All Saints' and All Souls' Days at All Saints', Lambeth, 1877	Rev. F. G. Lee, D.C.L.	159
Aurora	Rev. R. S. Hawker, M.A.	162
My Home	Miss Helen Montagu Stuart	165

"An arid plain, with rocky mountains lit,
From time to time, with sunshine, frowning by;—
Such was my path. Alone and solitary
I took my way. So lone it might have been
My last dread journey into Death's dark vale;
(For each one takes that journey all alone.)
Above, black clouds; around, the wailing wind;
While onward, o'er the level plains of sand,
No streak of silver heralded the Day.
Yet on the wind, when o'er me darkest night,
There came glad words with music weird and faint,
LYRICS OF LIGHT AND LIFE,—angelic strains
Echoed from Home on Earth or Home above,
To speed a footsore Wanderer on his way."

        "The Sorrows of Sewallis."

Lyrics of Light and Life.

BELOW AND ABOVE.

OWN below, the wild November whistling
    Through the beech's dome of burning red,
And the Autumn sprinkling penitential
    Dust and ashes on the chestnut's head.

Down below, a pall of airy purple,
    Darkly hanging from the mountain side,
And the sunset from his eyebrow staring
    O'er the long roll of the leaden tide.

Up above, the tree with leaf unfading
    By the everlasting river's brink,
And the sea of glass, beyond the margin
    Never yet the sun was known to sink.

Below and Above.

Down below, the white wings of the sea-bird,
    Dash'd across the furrows dark with mould,
Flitting with the memories of our childhood
    Through the trees now waxen pale and old.

Down below, imaginations quivering
    Through our human spirits like the wind,
Thoughts that toss like leaves about the woodland,
    Hopes like sea-birds flash'd across the mind.

Up above, the host no man can number,
    In white robes, a palm in every hand;
Each some work sublime for ever working,
    In the spacious tracts of that great land.

Up above, the thoughts that know not anguish,
    Tender care, sweet love for us below,
Noble pity free from anxious terror,
    Larger love without a touch of woe.

Below and Above.

Down below, a sad mysterious music,
    Wailing through the woods and on the shore,
Burdened with a grand majestic secret
    That keeps sweeping from us evermore.

Up above, a music that entwineth,
    With eternal threads of golden sound,
The great poem of this strange existence,
    All whose wondrous meaning hath been found.

Down below, the Church to whose poor window
    Glory by the autumnal trees is lent,
And a knot of worshippers in mourning,
    Missing some one at the Sacrament.

Up above, the burst of Alleluia,
    And (without the sacramental mist
Wrapt around us like a sunlit halo)
    The great vision of the Face of Christ.

Below and Above.

Down below, cold sunlight on the tombstones,
    And the green wet turf with faded flowers;
Winter roses, once like young hopes burning,
    Now beneath the ivy dripped with showers.

And the new-made grave within the churchyard,
    And the white cap on that young face pale,
And the watcher, ever as it dusketh,
    Rocking to and fro with that long wail.

Up above, a crowned and happy spirit,
    Like an infant in the eternal years,
Who shall grow in love and light for ever,
    Ordered in his place among his peers.

O the sobbing of the winds of Autumn,
    And the sunset streak of stormy gold,
And the poor heart, thinking in the churchyard,
    "Night is coming and the grave is cold."

Below and Above.

O the pale and plashed and sodden roses,
    And the desolate heart that grave above,
And the white cap shaking as it darkens
    Round that shrine of memory and love.

O the rest for ever, and the rapture,
    And the Hand that wipes the tears away;
And the golden homes beyond the sunset,
    And the hope that watches o'er the clay!

WILLIAM ALEXANDER,
Bishop of Derry.

All Saints' Day, 1857.

MY BIRTHDAY.

LET the sun summon all his beams to hold
    Bright pageant in his court, the cloud-
        paved sky;
Earth trim her fields and leaf her copses cold;
    Till the dull month with summer-splendour vie.
    It is my Birthday;—and I fain would try,
Albeit in rude, in heartfelt strains to praise
    My God, for He hath shielded wondrously
From harm and envious error all my ways,
And purged my misty sight, and fixed on heaven
    my gaze.

Not in that mood, in which the insensate crowd
    Of wealthy folly hail their natal day,—
With riot throng, and feast, and greetings loud,
    Chasing all thoughts of God and heaven away.

My Birthday.

Poor insect! feebly daring, madly gay,
What! joy because the fulness of the year
   Marks thee for greedy death a riper prey?
Is not the silence of the grave too near?
Viewest thou the end with glee, meet scene for
      harrowing fear?

Go then, infatuate! where the festive hall,
   The curious board, the oblivious wine invite;
Speed with obsequious haste at Pleasure's call,
   And with thy revels scare the far-spent night.
   Joy thee, that clearer dawn upon thy sight
The gates of death;—and pride thee in thy sum
   Of guilty years, and thy increasing white
Of locks; in age untimely frolicksome,
Make much of thy brief span, few years are yet to
      come!

Yet wiser such, than he whom blank despair
   And fostered grief's ungainful toil enslave;

My Birthday.

Lodged in whofe furrowed brow thrives fretful care,
  Sour graft of blighted hope; who, when the wave
  Of evil rufhes, yields,—yet claims to rave
At his own deed, as the ftern will of heaven.
  In footh againft his Maker idly brave,
Whom e'en the creature-world has toffed and driven,
Curfing the life he mars, "a boon fo kindly given."[1]

He dreams of mifchief; and that brainborn ill
  Man's open face bears in his jealous view.
Fain would he fly his doom; that doom is ftill
  His own black thoughts, and they muft aye purfue.
  Too proud for merriment, or the pure dew
Soft gliftening on the fympathizing cheek;
  As fome dark, lonely, evil-natured yew,

---

[1] "Is life a boon fo kindly given?" &c. — Vide *Childe Harold*, cant. ii.

My Birthday.

Whose poisonous fruit—so fabling poets speak—
Beneath the moon's pale gleam the midnight hag
    doth seek.

No! give to me, Great Lord, the constant soul,
    Nor fooled by pleasure nor enslaved by care;
Each rebel-passion (for Thou canst) controul,
    And make me know the tempter's every snare.
    What, though alone my sober hours I wear,
No friend in view, and sadness o'er my mind
    Throws her dark veil?—Thou but accord this
        prayer,
And I will bless Thee for my birth, and find
That stillness breathes sweet tones, and loneliness
    is kind.

Each coming year, O grant it to refine
    All purer motions of this anxious breast;
Kindle the steadfast flame of love divine,
    And comfort me with holier thoughts possest;

My Birthday.

Till this worn body flowly fink to reft,
This feeble fpirit to the fky afpire,—
   As fome long-prifon'd dove toward her neft—
There to receive the gracious full-toned lyre,
Bowed low before the Throne 'mid the bright feraph
    choir.

J. H. N<small>EWMAN</small>.

Trinity College, Oxford.
  February 21, 1819.

A ROSE PLANT IN JERICHO.

AT morn I plucked a rofe and gave it Thee,
    A rofe of joy and happy love and peace,
    A rofe with fcarce a thorn :
  But in the chillnefs of a fecond morn
  My rofe-bufh drooped, and all its gay increafe
Was but one thorn that wounded me.

I plucked the thorn and offered it to Thee ;
    And for my thorn Thou gaveft love and peace,
    Not joy this mortal morn :
    If Thou haft given much treafure for a thorn,
    Wilt Thou not give me for my rofe increafe
Of gladnefs, and all fweets to me ?

My thorny rofe, my love and pain, to Thee
    I offer ; and I fet my heart in peace,

A Rose Plant in Jericho.

And reſt upon my thorn :
For verily I think to-morrow morn
Shall bring me Paradiſe, my gift's increaſe,
Yea, give Thy very Self to me.

CHRISTINA G. ROSSETTI.

THE SILVER ARMY.

"There is neither speech nor language: but their voices
are heard among them."

I.

RUTHLESSLY the bare bright wheel of antique Time goes round,
And Middle Age has set his foot on Youth's enchanted ground;
The port has waxed more stately, the brow has sterner grown,
The smile is touched with sadness, and the man feels more alone.

II.

Ah, me! the golden lovelocks are changing into grey,
For God's silver silent army, no man may keep at bay:

And since I may not frown you down, nor motion
    you away—
O silver, silent monitors! what is it ye would
    say?

III.

" Where is 'the purple light of love,' and where
    the creeds of youth?
The faith in Manhood's honour, the repose on
    Woman's truth?
The summer friendship vanished when the storm
    began to rave,
And false Egeria slumbers calmly in her village
    grave.

IV.

" Life's gambler! thou hast lost thy stake—and
    what is left but gloom?
The fairy palace of Romance transformed into a
    tomb.

Dry is now thy fountain, Numa!—gone the dreamy grotto life—
Where the glamour of the Nymph-land—lo! the cold decorous wife!"

v.

O silver silent multitude! These voices are not thine,
Thy glittering mail was forgëd by a Hand that is Divine:
Numa has still a trysting-place, Life's glory has not flown,
For holy wedlock's crownëd Queen reigns on Egeria's throne.

vi.

Still in my creed man's honour and woman's love abide—
The phantasy of Boyhood with that village maiden died.

The deep ſtrong heart of manhood, the worſhip of
    a life—
The ſtainleſs fame, the honoured name, theſe, theſe
    I gave my wife!

VII.

The chivalry of labour is toil for others done—
By the worker, not the dreamer, are the ſtar and
    mantle won;
Who works for home and country, for him God's
    angel ſings—
"O labourer worthy of thy hire—the aureole and
    the wings."

VIII.

O mother of my children, the ſilvery hoſts of
    God
Bear in their hands enchanters' wands, and not th'
    avenging rod:

They point unto the land youth deemed so very far
    away[1]—
But Heaven looks nearer to us when the hair is
    growing grey.

JOHN PURCHAS.

[1] "They shall behold the land that is very far off."—*Isaiah* xxxiij. 17.

THE BASILICA OF ST. MARK, VENICE.

STATELY palace of the Triune God,
A myſtic ſanctuary of gloom and gleam,
With marbled ſaints, where twinkling lamps are hung,
And joyful bells ring out with ſilvery tongue,
Telling how ſwiftly moves on old Time's ſtream,
And how great races knew th' avenging rod.
Nor Occidental rites are here alone,
Nor Oriental forms. Majeſtic ſongs
Of Mary, round Incarnate God's high Throne,
Sung by Her children, gathered nigh in throngs
Where ſtill repoſe the relics of Saint Mark.
Link of the Eaſt and Weſt, but One true Ark.

Nations! turn eaſtward in thy weſtern pride,
 Eaſterns look weſtward—Adria is bright!

The Basilica of St. Mark, Venice.

Blue waters sleep around, or, night-starred, glide
   Near shrines, 'mid Earth's dark desert, of God's
      Light.

In peace, Lord, may thy servant now depart,
   My wondering eyes have seen this heavenly sight,
And I would choose henceforth the better part:
   Grant it, O Christ, whene'er draws on the Night,
   After Earth's toil and moil, to where is light,
Lord, may thy servant then in peace depart!

FREDERICK GEORGE LEE.

Venice, *Nov.* 15, 1877.

A MAY CAROL.

IS this, indeed, our ancient earth?
　　Or have we died in sleep and risen?
　Has Earth, like man, her second birth?
Rises the palace from the prison?

Hills beyond hills ascend the skies;
　In winding valleys, heaven-suspended,
Huge forests, rich as sunset's dyes,
　With rainbow-braided clouds are blended.

From melting snows through coverts dank
　White torrents rush to yon blue mere,
Flooding its glazed and grassy bank,
　The mirror of the milk-white steer.

A May Carol.

What means it? Glory, fweetnefs, might?
    Not thefe, but fomething holier far—
Shadows of Him that Light of Light,
    Whofe prieftly veftment all things are.

The veil of fenfe tranfparent grows:
    God's Face fhines out, that veil behind,
Like yonder fea-reflected fnows—
    Here man muft worfhip, or be blind.

AUBREY DE VERE.

FROM THE CLOISTER.

A FRAGMENT.

[*The monk* JEROME *seated in the cloister.*]

TO have wandered in the days that were,
Through the sweet groves of green
Academé!
Or shrouded in the night of olive boughs,
Have watched the starry clusters overhead
Twinkle and quiver in the perfumed breeze—
That breeze which, softly wafted from afar,
Mingled with rustling leaves and fountain's splash,
The boyish laughter and the maiden's song.
Or couched among the beds of pale-pink thyme
That fringe Cephissus with his purple pools,
Have idly listened while sweet voices sung
Of all those ancient victories of love
That never weary, and that never die.

Of Sappho's leap, Leander's nightly swim,
Of wandering Echo, and the Trojan maid,
For whom all ages shed their pitying tears:
Or that fair legend, dearest of them all,
That tells us how the hyacinth was born.
Next to have mingled in the eager crowd
That, questioning, circled some philosopher:
Young eyes that glistened, and young cheeks that
    glowed
For love of Truth, the great Indefinite.
Truth—beautiful as seem the distant hills,
Veiled in soft purple-crags, whereon is found
No tender plant in the increviced rock,
But clinging lichen, and black shrivelled moss.—
So should day pass, till from the summer sky,
Behind the marble shrines and palaces,
The big sun sank, reddening the Ægean Sea.
So should life pass, as flows the clear brown stream,
And scarcely stirs the water-lilies' leaves.
Life here, methinks, is like to some canal,

From the Cloister.

Dull, measured, muddy, washing flowerless banks.
O sunny Athens! home of life and love!
Free, joyous life that I may never live!
Warm, glowing love, that I may never know.
Home of Apollo, god of Poetry!
Dear bright-haired god, in whom I half believe,
Come to me, as thou didst come to Semele,
Trailing across the hills thy saffron robe,
And catch me heavenward wrapped in golden mists.

   I weary of this squalid holiness;
I weary of these hot black draperies;
I weary of the incense-thickened air,
The chiming of the inevitable bells;
The chanting too!—can man be made for this—
To hold his tongue all day, and sing all night?

   My boyhood, hurried over, but once gone
For ever mourned—return for one short hour!
Friends of past days, light up these cloister walls

From the Cloister.

With your bright prefences, and ftarry eyes,
And make the cold grey vaulting ring again
With tinkling laughter — Ah, they come! they come!
I fhut my eyes, and fancy that I hear
The funlit ripples kifs the willow boughs.

  But I forget myfelf; I muft confefs
All this to-morrow : thoughts—oh, let me fee !—
Of difcontent, and floth, and a diflike
To hear the clanging of the bleffed bells ;
And fomething elfe. Ah, well! all lovely things
That this vile earth affords—wood, mountain, ftream,
The regal faces, and the godlike eyes
We fee, the tender voices that we hear,
Are but mere fhadows : the reality
Is—what? A fomething up above the clouds.
From every carven niche the ftony faints
Stretch out their wafted hands in mute reproach ;

From the Cloifter.

And from the Crucifix, the great wan Chrift
Shows me His bleeding wounds and thorny crown.
Then, hark! I hear from many a lonely grave,
From blood-ftained fands of amphitheatres,
From loathfome dungeon, and from blackened ftake,
A cry—the martyrs' cry—" Behold the Man!"

   I hate myfelf, I hate this myftery,—
The dread neceffity of fuffering.
Is there no place in all the univerfe
To hide me in? no little ifland girt
With waves to drown the echo of that cry,
" Behold the Man, the Man of Calvary"?

   [BROTHER FRANCIS *croffing the cloifter, fings.*]
  Sweeteft Jefu, Thou art He
     To Whom my foul afpires;
  Sweeteft Jefu, Thou art He
     Whom my whole heart defires.

From the Cloister.

To love Thee, oh the extafy,
  The rapture and the joy!
All earthly loves foon pafs away,
  All earthly pleafures cloy.

But whofo loves the Son of God
  Of love fhall never tire,
But through and through fhall burn and glow
  With Love's undying fire.

     [*He enters the chapel.*]
  DIGBY MACKWORTH DOLBEN.

DESECRATION.

A HOUSE of prayer once confecrate
To God's high fervice—defolate!
A ruin where once ftood a fhrine,
Bright with the Prefence all divine!
Tread foftly here! 'tis hallowed ground,
And faithful hearts ftill find around
Traces of things which once were here
In days of love and reverent fear.

This is no common fpot of earth,
No place for idle words or mirth;
Here ftreamed the taper's myftic light,
Here flafhed the waving cenfers bright,
Awhile the Church's ancient fong
Lingered thefe ftately aifles among,
And high myfterious words were faid
Which brought to men the Living Bread.

Desecration.

O shame on those who will not own
The ruined shrine God's altar throne!
What though long years have come and gone
Since the last rite was duly done,
Since the last Sacrament was given,
Since the last prayer went up to Heaven!
True, men have wrought its sad disgrace,
But still it is God's Holy Place.

O it is easy work to say
" A purer Faith, a Gospel day,
Put all such holy ground aside,
And count all Nature sanctified."
It is not hard to dogmatize
And preach of " superstitious lies;"
To mock at " priestcraft," and to search
For some pet text to curse the Church:

But it *is* hard to bear the jeer,
To have the World's cold-hearted sneer,

Defecration.

The sneer the World for ever flings
At holy men and sacred things.
Courage! who fight the Cross beneath
Must fight unto the very death!
Faith, Hope, and Love the World shall win
From self, from sacrilege and sin!

W. C<small>HATTERTON</small> D<small>IX</small>.

ON THE BAPTISM OF A CHILD.

Morning.

BABE, awake! the fun is high,
   See, its beams are in the fky;
   Warm it fhines 'mid cloudlet torn,
On thy bright baptifmal morn.

Wake thee! for the Church to-day
Yearns to greet thee on thy way;
Hark! the bells ring joyfully,
Holy welcome, babe, for thee.

Child of Adam! doft thou bear
Stain of fin on face fo fair?
Gift of God, oh! muft we fee
Sin's dark heritage in thee?

On the Baptism of a Child.

Wake thee from thy light repose!
Holy Church would thee enclose,
Thee within her arms would hold,
Make thee lamb of Jesu's fold.

Evening.

BABY sleep! the sun is low,
   Evening shadows come and go;
Sleep, for on thy gentle brow
Gleams the Cross of Jesus now.

Calm thou liest in thy cot,
All thy baby woes forgot;
Fair thy dress, thy face how fair,
God's own image thou dost bear.

On the Baptism of a Child.

In the still baptismal hour,
O'er thee fell the Spirit's power;
In the blest Thrice-Holy Name,
Thou art washed from sin and shame.

Brightest drops of heavenly dew,
Then refreshed thy soul anew;
Child of God thou art become,
Heir of His eternal Home.

'Neath the Cross His children fight,
Boldly they maintain the right;
Thou His banner must uphold,
And in His dear cause be bold.

Sleep thee, babe, beneath His care,
Angels to thy cot repair;
Holy Guardians of the night
Guide thy tender dreams aright.

On the Baptism of a Child.

We around will kneel and pray
That the blessings wrought this day,
May through life sustain thy soul
Till it reach the heavenly goal.

NORA BATT.

THE DEATH OF ERMENGARDE.

A FRAGMENT.

(A girl speaks.)

A SAD, sweet end—
She sat upon the threshold of her door:
A long night's pain had left her living still:
Her cheek was white; but trembling round her lips,
And dimly o'er her face diffused, there lay
Something that, held in check by feebleness,
Yet tended to a smile. A cloak, tight-drawn,
From the cold March-wind screened her, save one hand
Stretched on her knee, that reached to where a beam,
Thin slip of watery sunshine, sunset's last,
Slanted through frosty branches. On that beam
(It brightened well that faded hand), methought,
Rested her eyes, half-closed. It was not so:

The Death of Ermengarde.

For when I knelt and kissed that hand ill-warmed,
Smiling, she said, " The small unwedded maid
Has missed her mark ! You should have kissed the ring !
Full fifty years upon a widowed hand
It holds its own. It takes its latest sunshine !"
She lived through all that night, and died while dawned
Through snows Saint Joseph's morn.

AUBREY DE VERE.

INDIA'S DREAM.

INDUS.

BROTHER! after set of day
   'Neath your western stars I lay,
   And I looked on other bowers,
And I dreamed of dreaming flowers.
O how fair the garden-glades!
O how strange their central shades!
In the heart of leaf and bloom,
Lo! a solitary tomb.

ANGLUS.

I too see, but not in dream,
'Neath all stars a garden gleam;
All things fragrant, all things white,
There lie buried in the night.

India's Dream.

Wonder not that one should die,
One in garden-tomb should lie,
When thou mayst that garden scan
Made a tomb, the soul of man.

INDUS.

This life's captives break their chain,
And to sunlight pass again,
This life's captives hope—the grave,
Never has set free its slave.
O the vision of my head!
Empty was that garden-bed,
And a voice struck on my ear,
" He is risen! He is not here!"

ANGLUS.

I, not less, the winter flown,
See a vision like thy own,
When, from a dead life unseen,
Wave the fields with living green;

India's Dream.

I shall see, and thou, and all,
At the World's great funeral,
A true garden every tomb,
Whence the dead shall spring and bloom.

INDUS.

In the place where flowers blow
Gardeners pass to and fro;
One seemed set to dress and keep
The fair garden of my sleep.
O with wounded feet and hands
In the sunrise here He stands,
And I own Him, Seed, Sun, Showers,
Gardener of all God's flowers!

In the drought men water bring
Thirsty flowers watering:
I am thirsty; flood thou me
With the Christ of Calvary.

India's Dream.

ANGLUS.

In the Name of Father, Son,
And of Him, the Holy One,
Live—and light the ſtarleſs ſod;
England owes to Ind her God.

A. Middlemore Morgan.

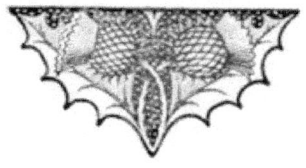

OUR REST.

NIGHT falls apace, the shades grow long
    Athwart the dewy lawn;
Blithe birds pipe out their evensong,
    Flowers close till welcome dawn.

Behind the hill-tops, sinking low,
    Passed the great Sun away;
Now paler spreads fair saffron glow
    Amid the deepening grey.

All seek repose when night is nigh—
    The tender doves their nest,
The lambs, safe-folded, sleeping lie,
    The babe on mother's breast.

Our Reſt.

So ſeek we, Lord, in Thee to reſt,
   Who lengtheneſt out our days,
Meet offerings bring—of prayer our beſt,
   And ſweeteſt ſongs of praiſe.

Care fills our lives—our cares on Thee
   We caſt from day to day:
Thy Voice ſounds gently "Come to Me
   Who bare your ſins away."

Weak are our footſteps—Thine the power
   To raiſe us when we fall;
Full oft we ſtray in evil hour,
   Do Thou our ſouls recall!

What if we loſe Thee? whence our hope?
   Who elſe can ſave or cheer?
Dread were our doom unhelped to grope
   In blank deſpair and fear.

Our Reſt.

But Thou art ours—True ſtrength and ſtay ;
   At morn our Bread of Life ;
Until the cloſing of Life's day
   Our Peace 'mid toil and ſtrife.

Be with us, Jeſus, at the end,
   When death-ſhades round us cloſe,
Light in our gloom in pity ſend,
   And grant a ſweet repoſe.

E. Louisa Lee.

THE SISTER OF MERCY.

I.

SHE was his playmate when a child: and, in Life's golden hours,
He loved her as he loved the ſtars, as he loved the ſtarry flowers;
With crown of flowers he dowered her, and all the wealth of May,
And ſhe was his dream-angel by night and his fairy-queen by day.

All day ſhe was his fairy-queen, her realms of fairy light
Were the wild woods beautiful with flowers, and the ſun-kiſſed mountain height,

The Sister of Mercy.

And the heather on the upland, and the shingle by the sea,
And wherever she went was fairy-land, and her own true knight was he.

All night she was his dream-angel; no crown of flowers was there,
But a crown of starry glory beamed around her golden hair,
And not the sunny smile of day beneath that cross of light,
But a dreamy starry smile, like the smile of dewy Night.

And often when in boyish glee he prattled fast and wild,
A strange, weird awe would mingle with his love for that fair child;

And he ceaſed his childiſh talk, and a ſhadow on him lay,
For ſhe ſeemed as though ſhe heard him not, and her heart was far away.

He ſaw her once at eventide: the glorious ſun went down,
And kiſſed her golden treſſes as with an angel's crown,
And it lay upon her pale white face, and radiant brow upraiſed,
And he ſaw his own dream-angel, and trembled as he gazed.

He knew his own dream-angel: thoſe eyes of heavenly love,
That dreamy ſtarry ſmile beneath the kindling ſkies above;

And it burst upon his heart, like a flash of awful light,
And she was his fairy-queen no more but his dream-angel of Night.

II.

SHE knelt before the altar in bridal robes of white ;
The church was beautiful with flowers, and blazed with starry light ;
There were flowers above the altar, and flowers wreathed in her hair,
And angels gazed upon her brow, and saw a star-crown there.

She knelt before the altar: the organ pealed on high,
They swelled the wedding hymn of joy up to the listening sky,

And angels' harps caught up the strain, and pealed it far away,
For God Himself comes down to claim a fair young bride to-day.

He saw his own dream-angel: the glorious sunlight came,
And kissed her virgin forehead with a crown of gold and flame;
And it lay upon her snowy flowers and on her golden hair,
But he was kneeling far away in sorrow and despair.

Strange strength arose within his soul: he let no teardrop start,
He checked each wild rebellious sob that trembled at his heart;

And he said: "O God, I loved her more than all
    the world beside,
But now Thy Will, Thy Will be done: I covet
    not Thy Bride.

"I was not worthy of her love, this sinful heart of
    mine,
Of that pure virgin heart of hers, where every throb
    was Thine;
I was not worthy of her love; and give her up to
    Thee,
And Thou wilt hear her, if perchance she pray one
    prayer for me."

The last sweet hymn has died away: the awful rite
    is o'er,
And she is now a Bride of Christ, His love for
    evermore:

And he bore his sorrow meekly, but his life had lost its light,
And she was his fairy-queen no more, but his dream-angel of night.

III.

HE lay upon the battle-field . . . . with faint and gasping breath,
Among the dying and the dead, on that grim field of death:
And no sweet hymn went up to God to soothe his aching head,
But the moaning of the dying and the wailing for the dead.

He lay upon the battle-field, and on his fevered brain,
A thousand memories of the past came rushing back again;

His father and his mother, and the cottage by the lea,
And the chair where firſt he ſaid his prayers beſide his mother's knee:

And then his mother ſmiled on him, and tears were in his eye,
But he knew not why he wept for her, nor what it was to die;
And the dance of his young life went on with all its joy and pain,
But he never ſaw his mother's ſmile, nor felt her kiſs again.

The wild woods and the leaping brooks, and a little child at play,
A little blue-eyed, fair-haired child, with a crown of early May;

And her crown became a crown of stars, and her
    star-crossed brow grew bright,
And she smiled a dreamy starry smile, like the smile
    of dewy night.

An altar bright with lights and flowers, and a fair
    girl kneeling there,
And a breaking heart, and a stifled moan, and a
    faintly-whispered prayer,
And the moaning of the dying and the wailing for
    the dead,
And his own dream-angel's gentle arm around his
    drooping head.

He started from his reverie, and kneeling by his
    side
He saw his own dream-angel, and so in peace he
    died ;

While her prayers for him went up to God beneath
    the stars all night,
And the Heavenly Bridegroom heard His Bride . . .
    and now he sleeps in light.

              FOLLIOTT S. PIERPOINT.

THE OTHER SIDE.

"And when the even was come, he faid unto them, Let us pafs over unto the other fide."—St. Mark iv. 35.

HE day was done: befide the fultry fhore
    The cooling fhadows kiffed the reftlefs fea,
The words of wondrous wifdom now were o'er
    That make thy waves fo facred, Galilee!

The thronging multitude from far and nigh
    In eager hafte around His barque had preffed,
And, as He fpake, the hours paffed ftealthy by,
    And many a weary heart found peace and reft.

And then, as gently fell the evening dew,
    And the long day, with all its toil, was o'er,
The Mafter faith unto His chofen few,
    "Let us pafs over to the further fhore."

The Other Side.

So, when our day is ended, and we ſtand
    At even by the marge of Jordan's tide,
O may we firmly graſp His piercèd Hand,
    And paſs triumphant to the " other ſide."

ROBERT H. BAYNES.

WHITE IS THE COLOUR OF ANGELS.

"All glorious hues are in the pure white beam."
KEBLE.

WHITE is the colour of angels
  And of innocent virgin souls;
White is the orbëd night-queen
  In the purple sky that rolls.

White is the hue of gladnefs,
  And of hearts that know not grief;
White is the hue that Sadnefs
  Aye looks to for relief.

Down from the liquid heaven
  In myftic order laid,
The white ftars rain at even
  White joys that ne'er can fade:

White is the Colour of Angels.

For they rain on the folemn fpirit
    Mufing on things above,
On the realms that we inherit
    White with Eternal Love.

White in the Eafter feafon
    And at Chriftmas' time of joy,
Our Mother for loving reafon
    Ordaineth to employ.

White in the lovely May-tide
    Burfteth from every bufh;
White in the face of beauty
    Frameth a maiden blufh.

White is the noon-tide glory
    Blanching the diftant hills;
White on the ocean hoary
    The ftorm-toffed furges fills.

White is the Colour of Angels.

White are the fields at even
    When the fresh dew on them lies;
White is the verge of heaven,
    Ere the sun begins to rise.

I loved a white-browed maiden
    Arched o'er with gold-brown hair,
And eyne with brightness laden
    As the brightness of summer air.

O colour of white, I love thee!
    For ever amid my dreams
The shadow of white-winged angels
    To guard me with watching seems.

GEORGE AKERS.

OUR LADY OF THE SNOWS.

I.

THE World is very foul and dark,
    And ſin has marred its outline fair;
But we are taught to look above
    And ſee another image there!
And I will raiſe my eyes above,
    Above a World of ſin and woe,
Where ſinleſs, griefleſs, near her Son
    Sits Mary on a Throne of ſnow.

II.

Mankind ſeems very foul and dark
    In ſome lights that we ſee them in;
Lo! as the tide of life goes by,
    How many thouſands live in ſin!

But I will raife my eyes above,
　　Above the World's unthinking flow,
To where, fo human, yet fo fair,
　　Sits Mary on her Throne of fnow.

III.

My heart is very foul and dark,
　　Yes, ftrangely foul fometimes to me
Glare up the images of fin,
　　My tempter loves to make me fee.
Then may I lift my eyes above,
　　Above thefe paffions vile and low,
To where, in pleading contraft bright,
　　Sits Mary on her Throne of fnow.

IV.

And oft that Throne, fo near our Lord's,
　　To Earth fome of its radiance lends;
And Chriftians learn from her to fhun
　　The path impure, that hell-ward tends:

Our Lady of the Snows.

For they have learnt to look above,
    Above the prizes here below,
To where, crowned with a starry crown,
    Sits Mary on her Throne of snow.

v.

Blest be the whiteness of her Throne
    That shines so purely, grandly there,
With such a passing glory bright,
    Where all is bright, and all is fair!
God, make me lift my eyes above,
    And love its holy radiance so,
That, some day, I may come where still
    Sits Mary on her Throne of snow!

B.

"LET THE HILLS HEAR THY VOICE."

THE sun shines bright and glorious, and the hill tops are illumed
With a more than common light the day Our Lady was assumed;
For her the cloudless blaze of noon on the lonely tarn is glowing,
And the many-sounding torrents chant her praises in their flowing.

For her the golden valleys thick with cornfields laugh and sing,
And with voices of innumerous birds the happy woodlands ring;
The air is tremulous with song, and a preternatural motion
Stirs the deep music of the waves in sunless caves of Ocean;

"Let the Hills hear Thy Voice."

And the sound of many waters with accord of solemn mirth,
Like a worship without words, goes up inceffant from the earth,
The Magnificat of mountain-ftreams, and—sweeteft after fhowers—
An odour as of frankincenfe, wafted from myrtle bowers.

And shall we alone, dear Mother, when all around is gay,
Stand mute amid the tuneful choir that hails thy triumph day?
Nor heed the skylark's matin hymn, flooding the heavens with praife,
Faint echo of their angel harps who on thy brightness gaze?

Shall thy children raise no anthem, all unaudienced though it be,

"Let the Hills hear Thy Voice."

With the living rock for temple, and the far-
resounding sea,
Rolling organ notes of jubilee, responsive to their
song,
For the Mother of the Holy One, the Merciful, the
Strong?

What if there were who loved to roam those breezy
fern-clad hills,
And to dream away the summer nights beside their
tinkling rills;
Who thought to seek the beautiful in Earth's most
beauteous places,
While the mountain breath was fraught for them
with more than earthly graces;

Who revelled in the warm sunshine on lake and
flowery lea,
While Nature through her sweet constraints was
drawing them to thee?—

"Let the Hills hear Thy Voice."

O speed them home, dear Mother-Maid, who linger on the way,
Lighten their eyes who cannot see, and turn the feet that stray!

Guide thou their weary steps through days of anguish and unrest,
Through the darkness that is felt of doubts unconquered, unconfest,
To the land beyond the Eastern hills, lapt in the living ray
Of the Uncreated Vision, where the shadows flee away!

HENRY NUTCOMBE OXENHAM.

THE SERVANT OF CHRIST.

"He that is called, being free, is Chriſt's ſervant."
1 *Cor.* vii. 22.

I.

THY Hands have made me! in ſoul-ſaving flood
Thy Heart poured forth for me its precious Blood,
And Thy ſweet Breath gave me its Life Divine;
Therefore, my God and Saviour! I am Thine!

II.

Thine by the mighty Maker's matchleſs art,
Thine by the Paſſion of His broken Heart,
Marked on my brow with the ſin-ſcaring ſign,
My God! my Saviour! ſoul and body Thine!

III.

Slave of my passions, by Thy Love set free,
Bound in eternal servitude to Thee,
Thy right in me yielded with glad accord,
The slave of Christ—the freeman of the Lord.

IV.

O glorious Love! that takes that outcast Name,
Once the sad sign of suffering and of shame,
And makes it, when for Christ man doth it bear,
Than Royal titles freer and more fair.

V.

Therefore, to render up to Thee above,
All the deep tender passion of my love,
All the poor service that Thou wouldst employ,
Is not alone my duty, but my joy!

The Servant of Christ.

VI.

And whatsoe'er I do, Lord! let it be
Done from the heart—with single eye to Thee:
My purest motive, and my best reward,
To be Christ's slave!—the freeman of the Lord!

JOHN S. B. MONSELL.

GOLDEN RAYS.

"Through Life's long day and death's dark night,
O gentle Jeſu, be our Light."
F. W. Faber.

I.

WHEN tempeſts ceaſe at cloſe of day,
  And evening is ſerene,
  How welcome falls the golden ray
  O'er paſtoral valleys ſeen—
As 'twere a meſſage ſent to cheer,
By miſſioned angels lingering near.

II.

For, if a blinding miſt of tears
  Awhile obſcured our ſight,
The ſadneſs of long-vaniſhed years
  Seems like a dream of Night.

When, drawing near to Jordan's tide,
Glory illumes the other fide.

III.

The other fide? What tongue may tell
    That orient blufh of Morn
Tinging the facred lilies' bell,
    And rofes without thorn.
Oh that we had thy wings, fair dove,
To foar and reft in bowers above!

IV.

The peace which this World cannot give
    And cannot take away
Is found when faithfully we ftrive
    God's precepts to obey:
Prepared to breaft the awful flood,
Supported on the Holy Rood.

Golden Rays.

v.

O wondrous mercy, thus to deign,
    And offer lasting rest,
From sorrow, weariness, and pain,
    On gentle Jesu's breast:
So may our Alleluias sweet
Adore the Blessed Paraclete!

C. A. M. W.

DREAMS.

I.

S childhood wanes our dreams become lefs fair—
 Heaven has gone farther off—the child is dead:
When Manhood dawns upon us, it doth fcare
 God's Mother from her watch befide our bed;
For I believe that o'er an infant's fleep
Our Lady doth a gentle vigil keep.

II.

Thus a child's flumber is a holy thing;
 It deems its mother's kifs upon its brow
Is the foft glancing of an Angel's wing.—
 Ah! I have no fuch graceful fancies now!
Therefore I hold, hearing of one who can
Dream like a little child,—Heaven loves that man.

JOHN PURCHAS.

"IN HOC SIGNO VINCE."

N the ancient ſtory,
    Once a warrior high
    Saw a Croſs of glory
  Flaming in the ſky;
While around it reaching,
  Writ by Hand Divine,
Ran the holy teaching,
  "Conquer by this ſign."

World and fleſh and devil
  Seek our deadly loſs,
We muſt fight with evil
  Strengthened by the Croſs;
Thus our might renewing
  By the ſymbol bleſt,
"Faint but yet purſuing"
  Chriſt ſhall give us reſt.

"*In hoc signo vince.*"

Sign of our salvation
   Printed on the brow,
Ever fresh relation
   Of a solemn vow,
May we always love thee
   As our joy and pride,
Looking still above thee
   To the Crucified.

In the time of sorrow
   Peaceful we shall be,
Since from it we borrow
   Lessons, Lord, of Thee:
In the days of gladness
   We shall do Thy will,
For Thy Cross of sadness
   Keeps us humble still.

Till the cord is broken
   Of our earthly part,

" In hoc ſigno vince."

Let us wear the token
    Near a loving heart :
When the eye is glazing
    With the final ſtrife,
Still upon it gazing
    Paſs from death to Life.

ANGELUS DOMINI.

A PICTURE BY B. FRA ANGELICO.

PRESS each on each, sweet wings, and roof me in
   Some closèd cell to hold my weariness—
Desired, as from unshadowed plains, to win
   The palmy gloaming of the oasis.

Soft wings, that floated ere the sun arose,
   Down pillared lines of ever-fruited trees,
Where through the many-gladed leafage flows
   The uncreated noon of Paradise.

Still wings, in contemplation oftentime
   Stretched on the ocean-depth that drowns desire,
Where lightening tides, in never-falling chime,
   Ring round the Angel isles in glass and fire.

Angelus Domini.

From meadow lands that sleep beyond the stars,
    From lilied woods and waves the Blessed see,
Pass, bird of God, all pass the golden bars,
    And in thy fair compassion pity me.

O for the garden-city of the Flower,
    Of jewelled Italy the chosen gem,
Where angels and Giotto dreamed a tower
    In loveliness of New Jerusalem.

For these, when roseate as a wingëd cloud
    Upon the saffron of the paling East,
A glowing pillar in the House of God,
    That tower arose, the very loveliest:

Then shaking wings and voices there that sang
    Pass up and down the chaféd jasper wall,
And through the crystal traceries outrang,
    As when from height to deep the seraphs call.

Angelus Domini.

O for the valley-slopes which Arno cleaves
    With arrowy heads of gold unceasingly,
Parting the twilight of the grey-green leaves,
    As shafted sun-gleam on a rain-cloud sky.

For there, more white than mists of bloom above
    When sunset kindles Luni's vineyard height,
Strange presences have paced the olive grove,
    And dazed the cypress cloister into light.

But not for me the angel-haunted south—
    I spread my hands across the unlovely plain,
I faint for beauty in the daily drouth
    Of beauty, as the fields for August rain.

Yet hope is mine against some eastern dawn,
    Not in a vision, but reality,
To see thy wings, and, in thine arms upborne,
    To rest me in a fairer Italy.

DIGBY MACKWORTH DOLBEN.

THE CHILD'S OFFERING.

WAS feſtal day in Heaven,
    And many a ſeraph came
  With many a coſtly offering
    To bleſs the Eternal Name.

On never-tiring wings
    Of burning love they flew,
Cleaving their eager upward way
    Through the cærulean blue.

Swift as the lightning's ray,
    Which from the fartheſt Eaſt
Darts forth a beam of radiant flame
    Unto the fartheſt Weſt:

So, ſwiftly from each realm
    Of wide Creation's bound,
The willing vaſſals gladly throng
    The dazzling throne around:

The Child's Offering.

Each meekly veils his face
    Beneath the ſhadowing wing,
Before the awful Majeſty
    Of the Everlaſting King:

Each bearing to his Lord
    Some mark of tribute meet;
Some ſplendid ſervice, to be laid
    Low at his Sovereign's feet.

One brings a virgin world,
    Whoſe habitations fair
And ſinleſs, happy denizens
    Entruſted to his care,

He has preſerved from harm—
    Has trained in holy fear;
And now again reſigns his charge,
    Meet for the Viſion clear.

The Child's Offering.

One leads in ponderous chains
    A countlefs hoſt of hell
Whom he has vanquiſhed in the fight
    With Lucifer who fell.

One tells that he has hung
    In diſtant fields of space
A galaxy of rolling ſuns
    For angels' dwelling-place.

One wakes to a new ſtrain
    The muſic of the ſpheres;—
Rich harmonies till now unheard
    E'en by celeſtial ears.

Then all in chorus join,
    Raiſing a lofty ſong;—
A theme of praiſe which never yet
    Has fired archangel's tongue.

The Child's Offering.

Yet, 'mid the shining train
   Of bending Cherubin,
Is one whose offering prevails
   A special grace to win:

He brings no spotless world,
   No spoils of victory;
He leads not with his voice or harp
   The minstrelsy on high:

He bears no royal gift
   Nor costly sacrifice;
Of paltry worth it would be held
   If weighed at this World's price:

Yet 'tis as rich and rare,
   In sight of Heaven's King,
As all the trophies of success
   Which flaming seraphs bring.

The Child's Offering.

'Tis the firſt heavenward throb
 Of a young heart's young love;
Its freſh, full tide of gratitude
 To Him Who dwells above.

Grateful as Spring's firſt flowers,
 Lovely as earlieſt dawn,
Precious as in a mother's eyes
 Her infant eldeſt-born;

Pure as the deep blue lake
 Which, 'neath the ſummer ſky,
Mirrors the azure and the gold,
 Unruffled by a ſigh:

So dear in Jeſus' ſight,
 So beautiful appears
The heart which gives itſelf to Him
 In childhood's opening years.

WILLIAM EDWARD GREEN.

A DREAM OF PARADISE.

N the myftic realm of flumber, in the quiet land of reft,
Came to me a radiant vifion of the Country of the Bleft ;
Angels, through the filvery moonbeams, gliding fwiftly from the fkies,
Brought to me from Eden's garden that fair Dream of Paradife.

Foremoft in a long proceffion, in her fhining raiment dreft,
Came the one who, through all ages, bears a name for ever bleft ;
Queen of Heaven ! Spotlefs Lily ! walking in refplendent light

Which no mortal eyes can fathom, in the boundless
    Infinite;
Blessèd Lady! Mother Glorious! dare I hope to see
    thy face
In the Land where none can enter, save through the
    redeeming grace
Of the Cross which gives us access into the Most
    Holy Place?

Those who in her steps had trodden, followed her, in
    robes of white;
Palms within their hands were waving, they were
    crowned with gems of light.

They were there, the martyr-maidens, who had con-
    quered in the strife;
They were there, the meek and patient, who had
    borne the Cross through life;
Ransomed from Earth's tribulation—safe for ever in
    the Fold;

A Dream of Paradise.

Paffing 'neath the pearly gateway,—walking in the ftreets of gold ;
And I heard their thrilling anthem floating o'er the cryftal fea—
" Unto Him Who hath redeemed us, Glory, Praife, and Honour be ! "

But the dazzling vifion faded—it was far too bright to ftay ;
In the rofy tints of dawning vanifhed the celeftial ray.
Earthly chains are ftill around us, mortal prayers we ftill muft pray,
Pilgrims in the land of exile—waiting till the perfect day
Breaks upon the diftant mountains, and the fhadows flee away.

Helen Montagu Stuart.

THE BREAD OF LIFE.

WHEN by Thine altar, Lord, I kneel,
    And think upon Thy love,
O make my heart Thy goodnefs feel,
    Fix it on things above:
    My deareft Lord, when I retrace
      Thy wondrous love for me;
    Oh, how can I affection place
      On anything but Thee?

About to leave this wretched Earth,
    On man Thy thoughts ftill bent,
Thy facred boundlefs love gave birth
    To this fweet Sacrament:
    My deareft Lord, when I retrace
      Thy wondrous love for me;
    Oh, how can I affection place
      On anything but Thee?

The Bread of Life.

O Manna, which my sovereign Lord
   In pity left for me,
Without this majesty adored
   What would this exile be?
      My dearest Lord, when I retrace
         Thy wondrous love for me;
      Oh, how can I affection place
         On anything but Thee?

A desert land of woe and care,
   A pilgrimage of strife,
Who could its griefs and trials bea
   Without this Bread of Life?
      My dearest Lord, when I retrace
         Thy wondrous love for me;
      Oh, how can I affection place
         On anything but Thee?

My soul here finds a sovereign balm—
   A cure for every grief,

The Bread of Life.

Mid care and pain a heavenly calm,
  A ſolace and relief.
    My deareſt Lord, when I retrace
      Thy wondrous love for me;
    Oh, how can I affection place
      On anything but Thee?

Supported by this Heavenly Bread,
  My Lord's laſt pledge of Love,
With joy the rugged path I'll tread
  To Horeb's mount above.
    My deareſt Lord, when I retrace
      Thy wondrous love for me;
    Oh, how can I affection place
      On anything but Thee?

Strengthened by this, my ſoul its flight
  Shall from this exile ſoar,
To dwell in realms of bliſs and light
  For ever—evermore.

The Bread of Life.

My dearest Lord, when I retrace
Thy wondrous love for me;
Oh, how can I affection place
On anything but Thee?

RIVER THOUGHTS.

ON RECEIVING FROM AN OLD AND DEAR FRIEND A BEAUTIFUL BOOK ON THE THAMES.

 TEMPLE,[1] backed with tree and based with turf,
Cresting the bright blue reach : — an ancient Lock,[2]
On whose worn gates the tiny wavelets knock
For entrance, and play round with mimick surf:

A Cell, once of religion—then of rakes,[3]
And now of pleasure-feastings underneath

---

[1] The Temple or summer-house on Fawley Island below Henley.
[2] Hambledon Lock.
[3] Medmenham Abbey—and its " Franciscans."

River Thoughts.

Old Trees, through which the river-breezes breathe,
And sound of voice and flute sweet music makes

From shallop, hasting homeward at grey eve:
White cliffs:[1] broad fall of waters at the Ford,[2]
Dove-cote, and Terrace-walk of soft green sward,[3]
Then an old Abbey,[4] where a Boy[5] would weave
Fancies[6]—afloat and drifting to and fro—
Wild fancies—that shall live while Thames' still
    waters flow.

    Such is the song that Memory sings
        To me of homes and hours gone by;
    A tale of ne'er-forgotten things;
        A record that will never die:

---

[1] Danesfield Cliffs.
[2] Harley-ford, its falls and foot-bridge.
[3] Hurley: Dove-cote and waterside walk, Lady-place.
[4] Bisham.   [5] Shelley.
[6] "The Revolt of Islam," under its past name, "Laon and Cythna."

River Thoughts.

Stirred by those seven sweet myftic strings
Up, from the inmost heart, it springs—
The thought—that all Life's bygone brings
    Back to the eye;
Old hearts, old haunts, old talks, old times,
Old Halls, old Towers, and old Church-chimes,
    Life's melody.

WILLIAM JOHN BLEW.

PURBROOK, HAMPSHIRE.

EASTWARD speed in gentle thought,
    And climb the steep Portsdown,
Then the meek rivulet be sought
    That winds beyond its crown:
As westwards tends the sunlight, round
    On church and hamlet look,
And muse how meetly this fair ground
    Is named from this Pure Brook.

This Brook is like the christened souls
    Who in fair Purbrook dwell;
The river-wave, the life-wave, rolls
    Each from a secret well;
But men may mark the streamlet's birth
    Where wild birds build and sing;
Who may trace back the Church on earth?
    Who shall declare its spring?

Purbrook, Hampshire.

Wilt trace it to the font's fair gleam,
    Pure water purified,
Pure water from an earthly stream
    Lost in a purer tide?
There with the Everlasting Years
    Is linked the life late given;
There is no eye of sun-lit spheres
    Gifted to pierce the Heaven.

Glassing the Sun upon its breast,
    Gladdening the neighbour soil,
The stream, scarce noticed, flows to rest,
    'Twixt the green banks of toil.
This is each faithful blood-bought soul,
    They who still heav'nward look
To seek their being's Fount and Goal,
    To lift their own Pure Brook.

A. Middlemore Morgan.

HYMN AFTER HOLY COMMUNION.

OH union wonderful and true!
    Oh, Love! oh, bliſs beyond compare!
What can the heart enraptured do
    When God Himſelf is there?

After communion what is earth?
    Life ſeems indeed but vanity:
Its brightest hours are never worth
    One moment ſpent with Thee.

This moment does the work of years,
    The ſoul hath drunk a joy ſo deep
That ſhe may bid farewell to tears,
    Such as Earth's children weep.

Jeſus! be Thou my hidden reſt,
    Reign over me ſupreme, alone;
The deareſt wiſh within my breaſt
    Is to be all Thine Own!

Hymn after Holy Communion.

And now, if to my daily ſtrife
   I muſt return, and bear my part;
Do Thou, my Lord, my Light, my Life,
   Keep to Thyſelf my heart!

Hold it, that it may never ſtray,
   Loſt in a World of ſin and care,
Fix it in the unerring way
   Of diſcipline and prayer.

Give me Thy bleſſing, Lord, again;
   And I will fight beneath Thine Eye,
And win, perchance, through days of pain,
   A glorious victory.

SALVE MI ANGELICE.

A HYMN FOR THE COMMEMORATION OF GUARDIAN ANGELS.

HAIL! my guardian spirit, hail!
    Angel ever blessed,
Who of light within the veil
    Throughly art possessed;
Thou of God Almighty hast
    Beatific vision,
Sweet for ever to the taste,
    Unalloyed fruition.

When the spirits proud were cast
    Into death undying,
Thee did God establish fast,
    Heavenly grace supplying:

Salve mi Angelice.

In His paths preſerved thee,
    Spirit true and tender,
And commiſſioned thee to be
    My weak ſoul's defender.

Therefore I with bended knee
    Bow myſelf before thee,
And upraiſing ſuppliantly
    Heart and hands, implore thee,
That, with ever-watchful art,
    Thou to-day wouldſt aid me,
Leſt the adverſary's dart
    Subtly ſhould invade me.

May my body from diſtreſs
    Be by thee protected,
Be all thoughts of wickedneſs
    From my mind rejected:

Salve mi Angelice.

Everywhere and always speed
    From the foe to hide me,
And in thought and word and deed
    Be at hand to guide me.

Cleanse all past and present faults
    From my mind's intention,
And, when evil next assaults,
    Grant thy intervention.
O console and care for me,
    Cherish me in trouble,
Purge, enlighten perfectly,
    And my zeal redouble.

Pray that I remission find
    Of the Judge's sentence,
So to share my joy of mind
    On my true repentance;

Salve mi Angelice.

Living as shall please Him best
   Unto my life's closing,
All my longings aye at rest,
   All on Him reposing.

In the hour of death, bestow
   Thy true consolation;
Shield me from the watchful foe,
   Bid me take my station,
Where the hosts of heaven among
   In God's courts attending,
I may join the praises sung
   To His Name unending.   Amen.

H. W. MOZLEY.

A LEGEND OF THE WEEPING WILLOW.

WHITE were the ſtairs of marble ſtone,
　　But whiter were His Feet,
　Flecked with the Blood that muſt atone
For the apple ſickly-ſweet ;
　　As He came down,
　　Each mocking clown
Aroſe the King to greet.

It was not yet the time of figs,
　　But trees were budding fair,
They ſtripped the lithe long willow-twigs,—
　　All things the crime muſt ſhare !—
　　　With rod and ſcourge
　　　Their guilt to purge
Whoſe ſins the Sinleſs bare.

And red ſtains mar the marble ſtone,
  And on the long green leaves
Are blood-drops, as the willow lone
  Still hangs its head and grieves
    By pool and flood,
    Where the pale blue bud
The wreath of Memory weaves.

B. MONTGOMERIE RANKING.

THE HOLY SOULS.

"The Souls of the righteous are in the Hands of God."

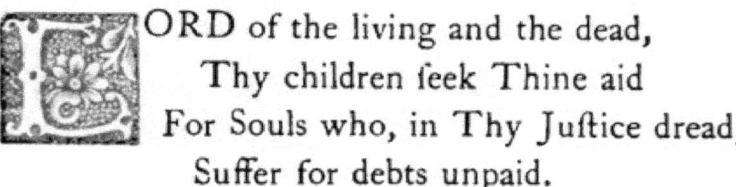ORD of the living and the dead,
    Thy children feek Thine aid
For Souls who, in Thy Juftice dread,
    Suffer for debts unpaid.

Shut out from Thee their one fole Love,
    They alway languifh fore
For cooling ftreams of blifs above,
    And Heaven's wide-opened door.

In twilight gloom they patient wait,
    Crofs-bearers of their Lord;
Stricken, until the prifon-gate
    Be opened at Thy word.

The Holy Souls.

Not yet so cleansed and purified
   That they may see Thy Face:
Not yet made meet, by suffering tried,
   For Thine all-pure embrace.

Yet Thou dost love them, and Thy love
   Is bliss amid their woe,
And for Thy sake the joys above
   They readily forego.

O then make haste, good Christ! and hear
   Our *De-profundis* cry;
Release the Souls, to Thee so dear,
   Who patient waiting lie.

Refresh them parched, with gracious rains—
   They long and thirst for Thee;—
Unloose their bonds, remit their pains,
   And set Thy captives free.

The Holy Souls.

Low at Thine altars here we bow,
   With tears Thy Paſſion plead,
The ſpotleſs Victim lifted now
   We offer for their need.

Soon give them welcome up above
   In Home of bliſsful reſt,
Fruition of Eternal Love,
   And ſight of Viſion bleſt.

E. Louisa Lee.

THE TROUVÈRE.[1]

 MAKE not songs, but only find:—
 Love, following still the circling sun,
His carols cast on every wind,
 And other singer is there none!

I follow Love, though far he flies:
 I sing his song, at random found,
Like plume some bird of Paradise
 Drops, passing, on our dusky bound.

In some, methinks, at times there glows
 The passion of a heavenlier sphere:
These, too, I sing:—but sweeter those
 I dare not sing, and faintly hear.

AUBREY DE VERE.

---

[1] The Greeks called the poet "the Maker." In the middle ages, some of the best poets took a more modest title—that of "the Finder."

HYMN OF PRAISE.

(*Pſalm* cxlviij.)

PRAISE, O praiſe the Lord of Heaven,
　　Praiſe Him, praiſe Him in the height;
Sun and moon, for ever praiſe Him,
　　Praiſe Him, all ye ſtars and light.

Praiſe Him, praiſe Him, all His angels,
　　Praiſe Him, praiſe Him, all His hoſt:
Praiſe the God of our Salvation,
　　Father, Son, and Holy Ghoſt!

Praiſe Him, praiſe Him, all ye Heavens,
　　And ye waters, that above,
From your everlaſting fountains,
　　Riſe in light and fall in love.

Hymn of Praise.

Praiſe Him, all ye deeps and dragons
    Upon earth, praiſe ye the Lord;
Fire and hail and ſnow and vapour,
    Wind and ſtorm, fulfil His Word.

Praiſe Him, all ye hills and mountains,
    Cedars fair and fruitful trees,
Beaſts and cattle, birds and inſects,
    Morning's light and evening's breeze.

Let them praiſe His Name Moſt Holy,
    For He ſpake and they were made,
Laws which never ſhall be broken,
    Deep in their foundations laid.

Kings below and all the people,
    Princes, judges of the earth,
Young and old men, maidens, children,
    Praiſe His Name of matchleſs worth.

110   *Hymn of Praiſe.*

For that Name, all names excelling,
   From His people's hearts ſhall raiſe
To His own eternal dwelling
   Endleſs ſongs of love and praiſe.

Praiſe, O praiſe the Lord of Heaven,
   Praiſe Him, praiſe Him in the height;
Sun and moon, for ever praiſe Him,
   Praiſe Him, all ye ſtars and light!

Praiſe Him, praiſe Him, all His angels,
   Praiſe Him, praiſe Him, all His hoſt:
Praiſe the God of our ſalvation,
   Father, Son, and Holy Ghoſt.

JOHN S. B. MONSELL.

THE SHIP IN THE STORM.

" The ſhip was now in the midſt of the ſea, toſſed with waves."

SAW " the waves of this troubleſome world," raging and dark and cold,—
Oh, who will guide in the ſtormy tide to reſt in the city of gold?
The Lord has been to our realms of ſin, and bought us in Heaven a ſhare,
But He is gone back on the angel's track, and how ſhall we reach Him there?
Then a glance I caſt through the long, long paſt; (its viſta was nearly dark,)
And, through the haze of vaniſhed days, diſcerned a noble barque
Which the " Carpenter's Son," that fearleſs One, had built with His own right hand,
And in her thoſe dear to His Heart while here, embarked for their Fatherland.

The Ship in the Storm.

The Workman is gone, yet crowds preſs on to that fruit of His toil unpriced;
All bear the ſign of Love Divine, the holy Croſs of Chriſt.
The ſame ſweet Light through ſtorm and night is guiding all to reſt,
And, hand-in-hand, to toil for land, they ſhould be ſurely bleſt.
But ſome cannot view the lantern true, and to them all days are dark;
Some proudly rear, and think as clear, their candle's little ſpark.
Some try to wile the brief ſummer's ſmile for ever there to roam,—
Alas! to ſuch is the voyage much, and little worth their home.
Some look for light with aching ſight, and tremble day by day,
Leſt, though they ſtrive to ſafe arrive, they ſhould be caſt away.

The Ship in the Storm.

Some leave the reſt, and boldly breaſt alone the open wave,
And many die from far and nigh, and find an ocean grave;
Like drops of rain on the ſtormy main, their place is known no more,—
O death and life! O toil and ſtrife! when will this ſcene be o'er?

Y. N.

CORPORATE REUNION.

 LORD, we know that all who love Thy Name
    Are one in Thee; Thy Spirit's quickening fire
Has wrapt their torpid nature into flame,
    And given them oneness of intense desire
    To mount towards Thee higher still and higher.
Yet are they widely severed to their shame
    In outward worship: discord in the choir
Brings on their glorious Faith the sceptic's blame.
O turn we, therefore, schism-torn to Thee,
    And ask that Thou wouldst make us whole again,
Not only in the Spirit's unity,
    But in a visible communion;—then
The Holy Catholic Church indeed will be
    Thy home, Thy tabernacle among men.

                        JOHN CHARLES EARLE.

Visitation of B. V. Mary, 1878.

SUPER FLUMINA.

THE vesper bell is pealing soft,
    And I know that, far away,
The vesper hymn goes up aloft,
    To lull the dying day;
And a gentle Child on bended knee
Is pouring forth a prayer for me.

Pray, gentle spirit, far away,
    By that sweet southern sea;
I have need enough that day by day
    Some prayer should rise for me,
Some incense to the eternal shrine,
From heart and lips as pure as thine.

I scarce could pray an hour ago,
    A weight was on my heart,

But now it melts like morning snow,
  And I can weep apart,
For thou art praying for me now,
And God will listen to thy vow.

Pray, gentle spirit; prayer of mine
  Is stained and flecked with earth,
But every snow-white prayer of thine
  Is rich with Angel's worth;
And mingling in the starry zone,
Those prayers shall purify mine own.

Sweet is the Ave-Mary bell,
  In Mary's land of love,
And sweet the vesper hymns that swell
  To Her dear Throne above;
And sweet to me far, far away,
The hour when Mary's children pray.

Adieu, sweet Child, adieu to-night!
  Christ keep thee safe from ill!

Super Flumina.

Thy dreams be sweet, thy sleep be light,
    Good Angels guard thee still:
And God the Father from above
Smile on thee with a Father's love.

Folliott S. Pierpoint.

IMMACULATA.

COULD ſhe, that Deſtined one, could ſhe
    On whom His gaze was fixed for aye,
  Tranſgreſs like Eve, partake that Tree,
In turn the Serpent's dupe and prey?

Had He no Pythian ſhaft that hour,
    Her Son—her God—to pierce the Foe
That ſtrove her greatneſs to devour,
    Eclipſe her glories? Deem not ſo!

O Mary! in that Firſt Decree
    He ſaw the aſſailer, ſent the aid:—
Filial it was, His love for thee
    Ere thou wert born; ere worlds were made.

Immaculata.

One Innocence on earth remained
   By Grace divine, not Nature's worth,
And welcomed—through His Blood, unftained—
   Redeeming Sanctity to earth.

AUBREY DE VERE.

ANOTHER FLEETING DAY IS GONE.

ANOTHER fleeting day is gone,—
   Slow o'er the Weſt the ſhadows riſe;
Swiftly ſoft ſtealing hours have flown,
   And Night's dark mantle veils the ſkies.

Another fleeting day is gone,—
   Swept from the records of the year,
And ſtill with each ſucceſſive ſun
   Life's fading viſions diſappear.

Another fleeting day is gone,—
   When all who in God's care confide
As their appointed work is done,
   Reſt in His love at eventide.

Another fleeting day is gone,—
   But ſoon a fairer day ſhall riſe,

Another fleeting Day is gone.

A day whose never-setting sun
   Shall pour its light o'er cloudless skies.

Another fleeting day is gone,—
   All praise to God, as is most meet,
To God the Father, God the Son,
   And God th' all-holy Paraclete.   Amen.

I.

IN GOD'S SIGHT.

WHY should we vex our foolish minds
    So much from day to day,
With what concerning us an idle World
    May think or say?

Do we not know there sits a Judge,
    Before Whose searching eyes
Our inmost hidden being cleft in twain
    And open lies?

O my Omniscient Lord and God!
    Enough, enough for me,
That Thou the evil in me and the good
    Dost wholly see.

Let others in their fancies deem of me,
    Or say, whate'er they will,
Such as I am before Thy judgment-throne
    So am I still.

In God's Sight.

Praise they my good beyond desert,
    And all my bad ignore;—
That am I which in Thy pure sight I am,
    No less, no more!

Decry they all my good, and blame
    My evil in excess;—
That am I which in Thy pure sight I am,
    No more, no less!

EDWARD CASWALL.

"THY KINGDOM COME."

No. I.

HOW long, O Saviour, wilt Thou ſtay ?—
How long Thy ſure return delay ?
While ſtill Thy waiting Church doth pray
    "Thy kingdom come."

Didſt not Thou teach the prayer, O Lord ?
Haſt Thou not paſſed the faithful word ?
Oh ! gird Thee with Thy conquering ſword :
    "Thy kingdom come."

Are not the realms of Earth Thine own ?
Come, then, and ſtabliſh here Thy throne :
In all the World reign Thou alone :
    "Thy kingdom come."

"Thy Kingdom come."

Jesu! descend again from high;
And while Thine armies fill the sky
Let Earth resound, and Heaven reply:
　"Thy kingdom come."

Why lingereth Thy chariot still?
When wilt Thou all the nations fill
With the glad praise of Sion's hill?
　"Thy kingdom come."

Till then, oh! keep us in the way
Which leadeth to Eternal Day;
And grant us grace in faith to say:
　"Thy kingdom come."

WILLIAM EDWARD GREEN.

"THY KINGDOM COME."

No. II.

SAY not that hours are lonelier now and darker
    Than days were dark of yore,
Say not that wild winds moan old days' departure,
    For sunshine lights the floor:

Yes, golden sunshine creeps through pane and portal
    Up the dim wall,
Whence pictured faces look with smiling feature,
    And voices seem to call:

Sunshine of Earth, bright type of heavenly glory,
    Where come nor loss nor fears,—
Sunshine of Earth, flecked ever with dark shadows,
    In this sad vale of tears.

"Thy Kingdom come."

Round us such shades have deepened, paled the gloaming,
    Now Summer joys have fled,
Yet even in Winter come familiar greetings
    And memories of the dead.

Until we pass, in Spring, Life's June, or Winter,
    From this strange varying scene,
Bind us to those we loved, by living prayer-bonds,
    Lord, keep their memories green :

Grey hairs and deep-veined fingers, cold and death-struck,
    With *De profundis* sung,
Faces so white and calm, the struggle over,
    When chimes of hope were rung :

While round the death-biers little children fearful
    Gathered with smile and tear,

"Thy Kingdom come."

And little palms were joined in interceſſion
 For thoſe ſo loved and dear.

Paſt all the woes and ſufferings, o'er the ſtruggle,
 No more the trumpet-call:
Paſt all the toil and all the ſtrong temptation,
 No weakneſs now, no fall.

As pants the hart for cool refreſhing brooklets,
 When heated in the chaſe,
So long the ſouls, O Lord, of our departed
 To look upon Thy Face.

Patient and waiting for glad ſtreaks of ſunlight
 To ſcare dark miſts away,
Patient and waiting through the long night-watches
 For God's all-peaceful day.

There bonds long-ſevered, with ſad ſeparations,
 By His divine decree,

Shall be new-linked in that true home celeſtial
    Before the cryſtal ſea.

So when bright ſpring-flowers gild the glad green
        meadows,
    And birds rejoicing ſing,
Pray for the Reſurrection-morning's beauty—
    Look for the Church's King.

Or here, when Autumn's reddening touch ſo
        changeth
    Leaf, floweret-bloom, and lea,
Aſk we to tread the good God's garden homewards,
    And eat of Life's rich Tree.

We ſtill miſs friends, and grieve o'er their departure,
    Hands cold and voices dumb,—
Join us anew where ſeparations are not,
    O Lord, Thy Kingdom come!

"Thy Kingdom come."

So, as at sleeping-place, poor pilgrim-strangers,
 Thine Own loved Prayer we pray,
We look back from the empty tomb of Easter,
 On to the breaking Day.

FREDERICK GEORGE LEE.

THE TWO CROWNS.

MADE myself a myrtle crown;
    I crowned myself with leaves and
        flowers;
  All day I lay in rosy bowers,
All day till the sweet sun went down.

The myrtle withered on my head,
    My crown became a crown of pain,
    I could not pluck it off again,
With those dead leaves my heart seemed dead.

All night, all night, without relief,
    I wandered, while the stars were bright,
    I wandered all that weary night,
And all my soul was sick with grief.

But when then morning broke once more,
    And all the hills were rofy fair,
    I found a ruined chapel there,
I paffed the little chancel door:

The Holy Altar glittered cold,
    Altar and Crofs were broken all,
    The mofs was thick upon the wall,
The day-fpring tinged its tufts with gold.

I knelt before the broken fhrine,
    I could not fpeak for fobs and tears,
    I could not pray for wildering fears,
The ruin of that fane was mine.

Long, long I knelt in my defpair,
    But when the fun in heaven was high,
    A glory feemed to hover by,
I felt a Healing Prefence there.

The Two Crowns.

So, when my grief was calmer grown,
    I said, "My heart was dark within;
    O God, I sinned a deadly sin,
I sinned, to wear the myrtle crown."

I saw a Form of Beauty there,
    A Form of Beauty heavenly bright,
    A glorious Form of awful light,
A Form of Beauty fairest-fair.

I wept, and clasped His sacred Feet,
    I wept and kissed them, as I lay:
    He took my crown of pain away:
I wept, and all my tears were sweet.

Another crown I wear ev'n now,
    A sweeter crown than in those bowers,
    And part are Amaranthine flowers,
And part are thorns from His dear Brow.

FOLLIOTT S. PIERPOINT.

EVENTIDE.

WHISPER the angel voices foft and kind,
    More gentle than the fummer even's wind
        That murmurs playful o'er the deep,—
"Sleep, child of earth," they fay, "now take thy reft;
The twilight darkens in the glowing weft,
    Spirits around thee watch fhall keep."

Come floating on the breath of balmy air,
Sweet dreams of heaven, and of our loved ones there,
    For ever in their Father's keep.
And whilft ftill Night ftole on with filent tread,
Around me hovering, holy Angels faid,
    " He giveth His beloved fleep."

And comes anon, from yonder wooded hill,
The diftant murmur of fome hidden rill

That ripples down its ftony bed.
And yet again I hear the angels' fong,
By evening's dying breezes borne along,
 " Sleep, fleep, ftill darknefs reigns o'erhead.

" Reft, reft," I ftill hear wafted on the breeze,
That, fighing fadly through the fhadowy trees,
 Makes mufic always low and deep—
And comes once more the oft-repeated ftrain,
Re-echoed gently from yon darkening main,
 " He giveth His beloved fleep."

HEDLEY VICARS.

HYMN FOR ALL SAINTS' DAY.

WE give Thee thanks, O Lord our God,
    For all the Saints Thy path who trod—
    The path of pain, the path of death,
The path of Him Who triumpheth.

For they have braved the hour of ſhame,
The croſs, the rack, the cord, the flame,
The dagger and the cup of woe,
If only Jeſus they might know.

All this they counted not for loſs,
For they were ſoldiers of the Croſs:
They recked not of the grief or pain,
If only Jeſus they might gain.

He is their Saviour, He their Lord,
He their exceeding great reward;

Hymn for All Saints' Day.

Though loſt be all that fills our cares,
If Him they have, then all is theirs.

From us their forms have paſſed away—
Mere viewleſs ſpirits, mouldering clay—
Some live upon the life of fame,
Some leave no veſtige but a name.

But when ſhall ſound the trump of doom,
To call the tenants of the tomb,
A mighty army they ſhall ſtand,
Arrayed in white at God's Right Hand.

A mighty hoſt, to man unknown,
In glory ranged around the Throne;
He knows His own Who ruled the ſtrife—
Their names are in the Book of Life.

GERARD MOULTRIE.

THE GREAT CLOUD OF WITNESSES.

"Compaſſed about with ſo great a cloud of witneſſes."—St. Paul.

"I believe in the Communion of Saints."—*Apoſtles' Creed.*

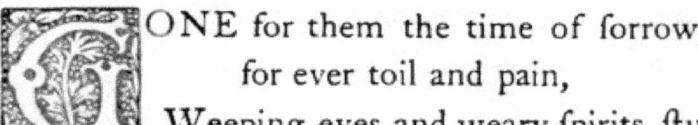ONE for them the time of ſorrow, paſſed for ever toil and pain,
Weeping eyes and weary ſpirits, ſtumbling feet, or moil or ſtain;
No more death nor ſin can touch them, they are ſafely folded now,
Great the guerdon of their patience, bright the crowns upon their brow.

Once, like us, they knew of weakneſs, of temptation's power, and ſhame,
But their God was near to help them, for they truſted in His Name;
So victoriouſly they triumphed, though, like us, in war they ſtrove,

Now they gaze upon His beauty, Who, like them, we ſtrive to love.

But, though rapt in ceaſeleſs worſhip, round the Lamb's high throne in light,
Though impaſſible exultant, bathed in fathomleſs delight;
Still from out the golden bulwarks, where the angels throng around,
Mark they well our faltering footſteps as we march through hoſtile ground.

Mindful are they of our victories when from ſin we turn away,
When, our burdens laid aſide, we walk as children of the day:
Yes, they yearn with love for ſinners, long to greet thoſe exiles dear,
And to ſhare with them the laurels when the fight is ended here.

Ask we then their prayers to aid us—know they not
    the gifts we need?
Who on earth being strong to battle, still are strong
    to intercede:
Filled while here with love's compassion, pity now
    for each they know;
Seek we then their willing succour, help to triumph
    o'er the foe.

He will hear them, Who has promised, "What ye ask
    ye shall receive;"
And His grace shall flow upon us who in His sure
    word believe;
Bound and bonded in communion with each other
    and the Trine,
Where the light is ever lustrous, and the peace is all
    divine.

The Authoress of "The Departed
and other Verses."

UNKNOWN GRAVES.

THE grafs is rank, the fhades are deep,
   Where the unknown their flumber keep,
   The early funlight, faffron-new,
Scarce fmites the grafs or gilds the dew ;—
Unprayed for, tended not, they wait,
Thofe Holy Souls, outfide God's Gate.

Beyond the Church's northern wall
Only day's noon-tide glories fall,
Here—dawn and morn, foft eve, dark night
Above—no change, unfading light ;
Yet round glide angel-guardians nigh
To hear a plaint and heed a figh.

No croffes mark thofe northern graves,
No flowers adorn, no yew-tree waves ;

Unknown Graves.

Unknown, uncared for, there they lie,
Under the chill of wintry sky,
Or, under light of July's sun,
Lorn and forgotten every one.

Pass no lone nameless sleeper's bed,
For once on such Heaven's dew was shed:
By sudden death, by wasting pain,
God called them to Himself again:
Pray then for Souls who longing wait
To enter Sion's golden gate.

The grass is rank, deep shadows lie
Under charged cloud or golden sky;
Not by the Church's southern plot
Where rose blooms with forget-me-not,
But for all Souls whose bodies rest
Under the northern churchyard's breast.

When chimes for mass ring out at morn
O'er snow-clothed vales or ripening corn,

Unknown Graves.

Gather within the open door
God's dews of mercy to implore
For Souls unknown, in Chrift new-born,
Waiting, unprayed for, lone and lorn.

FREDERICK GEORGE LEE.

Littlemore, September, 1874.

MANET SABBATISMUS.

WHEN man abode in Paradife,
　　There was in gardens once
　A perfect reſt defying price;
But man, ſo eager to be wiſe,
　　Hath proved himſelf a dunce,
　　　That toileth ſtill and ſtraineth:
　　And yet a reſt remaineth.

The ſerpent dwelt in Paradiſe,
　A good beaſt and a kindly,
But Satan coming, tempter-wiſe,
Filled all the poor beaſt's mouth with lies,
　　And Eve ſhe liſtened blindly;
　　　And living-kind complaineth:
　　And yet a reſt remaineth.

Manet Sabbatismus.

By wells of water, where the trees
   Bow down to kiſs the flowers
That, anchored, rock in morning breeze,
And ſpread their ſilver chalices
   To catch the morning ſhowers,
     No final reſt man gaineth :
     And yet a reſt remaineth.

In tender voice, in ſong of bird,
   In pſaltery's ſoft rhyming,—
So ſweet becauſe more felt than heard,—
   In ſound of kiſſes, timing
   The hours that aſk no chiming,
     There is no reſt : earth waneth :
     Only the reſt remaineth :

Remaineth in a garden-ground
   Where groweth Roſe and Lily,
Remaineth where the waters ſound,

Manet Sabbatismus.

Where never winds blow chilly,
Nor harsh voice echoes shrilly,
   Where the Rose-lily reigneth,
   There the true rest remaineth!

A little while, a little heat,
   A little loneliness,—
And endless time that grows more sweet,
   And warmth with no distress,
   And fellowship to bless
     His rest who rest obtaineth:
     The final rest remaineth.

B. M<small>ONTGOMERIE</small> R<small>ANKING</small>.

COMPLINE HYMN.

COME, bleſt Redeemer of the Earth,
Shew to the World a Virgin-Birth,
Let all the wondering ages know
Which birth beſeems our God below.

Not of the ſeed of mortal race,
By myſtic Breath of heavenly grace,
The Word of God, in fleſh arrayed,
True offspring blooms of Mother-maid.

The Virgin bears the Burthen pure,
And Ever-virgin doth endure;
Like pennon bright her graces ſhine,
And God is in His hallowed ſhrine.

The Bridegroom from His chamber ſprings,
Meet palace of the King of kings,
True God, true Man, in Perſon One,
Like giant glad His courſe to run.

148 *Compline Hymn.*

From Sire in Heaven He goeth forth,
To live in Heaven returns from Earth,
Descending e'en to Hell's abode,
Ascending to the Throne of God.

Eternal Sire's co-equal Son,
Thy fleshly girdle gird Thee on,
The frailty of our mortal plight
To strengthen with immortal might.

Full brightly shines Thy manger-bed,
And Night herself new light doth shed,
A Light on which no night shall close,
Aye bright to Faith as when it rose.

To God the Father in the height,
And to the Son, True Light of Light,
And Holy Ghost all glory be,
Now and through all eternity.   Amen.

LIGHT IN THE DARKNESS.

A CHRISTMAS CAROL.

THE blafts of chill December found
    The farewell of the Year,
And Night's fwift fhadows gathering round
    O'ercloud the foul with fear;
But reft you well, good Chriftian men,
    Nor be of heart forlorn:
December's darknefs brings again
    The light of Chriftmas morn.

The welcome fnow at Chriftmas-tyde
    Falls fhining from the fkies:
On village paths and uplands wide
    All holy-white it lies;

Light in the Darkness.

It crowns with pearl the oaks and pines,
    And glitters on the thorn;
But purer is the Light that shines
    On gladsome Christmas morn.

At Christmas-tyde the gracious moon
    Keeps vigil while we sleep,
And sheds abroad her light's sweet boon
    On vale and mountain-steep:
O'er all the slumbering land descends
    Her radiancy unshorn;
But brighter is the Light, good friends,
    That shines on Christmas morn.

'Twas when the World was waxing old,
    And Night on Bethlehem lay,
The Shepherds saw the heavens unfold
    A light beyond the day;

Light in the Darkness.

Such glory ne'er had visited
    A World with sin outworn;
But yet more glorious light is shed,
    On happy Christmas morn.

Those shepherds poor, how blest were they
    The angels' song to hear!
In manger cradle as He lay,
    To greet their Lord so dear!
The Lord of Heaven's Eternal height
    For us a Child was born;
And He, the very Light of Light,
    Shone forth that Christmas morn!

Before His infant smile afar,
    Were driven the hosts of hell;
And still in souls that childlike are
    His guardian love shall dwell:

Light in the Darkness.

O then rejoice, good Christian men,
    Nor be of heart forlorn;
December's darkness brings again
    The Light of Christmas morn.

Norval Clyne.

FOR A YOUNG GIRL WITH A BOOK OF CAROLS.

CAROL while yet thy life is in its spring,
    For spring-tide is the time for carolling:
    Sing while the dews are fresh, the day is young;
Sweet songs sound sweetest in the morning sung,
Ere yet the summer-noon, the winter-night
Harden the heart-springs, and the song-flowers blight;
And airs of youth and Carols "light as air"
Seem but the echoes of the things that were.
    Up! the sons of God are singing
        To the children of the plain;
    Up! the bells of Earth are ringing
        Back to Heaven their glad refrain:
    Up! the day-star forth is flinging
    Lines of golden light, and stringing

With a Book of Carols.

Beads of dew thereon, to deck
With Love's necklace Morning's neck:
Up! then, and on Music's string
Thread the pearls of song, and sing—
In a lone bower far away
There is born a Babe to-day!

WILLIAM JOHN BLEW.

REST.

"There remaineth, therefore, a rest for the people of God."

O TOILERS in Life's vineyard,
    Who sigh for perfect Rest,
    Whose dim eyes, peering upward,
With weight of years oppressed,
Look for the blissful slumber
    God gives to His beloved ;
Wait till the day is over,
    And He the task has moved.

Here, where the long long morning
    Melts into busy noon,
The hours are all unrestful,
    But Evening cometh soon :

Rest.

Lo on the lofty mountain
    The firſt faint ſhadow lies,
And God will draw His curtains
    Over the far-off ſkies.

Short ſlumbers has the pilgrim,
    His ready ſtaff in hand,
The ſoldier may but linger
    Till the foe is in the land :
The child muſt haſten homeward
    O'er hill and field and dell ;
And the golden gates are open
    Where they each in reſt ſhall dwell.

O weary heart, take courage !
    O feet, march on awhile !
O buſy hands, ſtill labour !
    Tired eyes ſhall ſee Him ſmile

Rest.

Who has within His keeping,
   Still waiting for your claim,
The perfect Rest of Heaven—
   The gladness of His Name.

No storm disturbs the waters,
   No wind shakes that repose;
No trumpet calls to battle,
   Nor triumph then the foes:
Though season follows season,
   And year fades into year,
That rest is still remaining—
   That Heaven shall still appear.

Take up the burden, Christian,
   Bear thou, and labour on,
A little sorrow only
   And the kingdom shall be won:

Rest.

  Only a few more footsteps,
    And then the tranquil Rest;
  Only a few more longings,
    And then the sheltering Breast.

ALL SAINTS' AND ALL SOULS' DAYS AT ALL SAINTS', LAMBETH, 1877.

MUSING over friends departed, loved ones known and miſſed and gone,
As November's ſun was ſmiling ſpeaking ſummer to the morn,
Autumn-blooms were ſweet and odorous in their lateſt parting breath,—
Yet gazing upon Beauty I could only dream of Death.

Golden ſhower-clouds drifting purpled up between the Earth and ſky,
Seemed to pauſe, as though thanks giving, ere like tears they fell to die;
Yet Earth in all its ſplendour was the goal where both were borne,

160 *All Saints' and All Souls' Days*

For I looked not so far onward as the Resurrection-
morn.

As All Saints' Night went gliding by, she wreathed
the sacred hours
With glory from her coronal of everlasting flowers:
There came, but not from Earth, a Voice that
whispered of the Blest,
An echo from that far-off land in which the wan-
derers rest.

The World had sobbed itself to sleep, all-silent after
strife ;
The shades of Death had vanished in the rays of
endless Life ;
While that Voice Divine thrilled sweeter from the
Home where angels soar,
As It whispered " Saints are shining as the stars for
evermore."

At All Saints', Lambeth, 1877.

While the Holy Souls are thirsting for our Eucharists
    and prayer—
Christ have pity! Lady help them! Mount they soon
    the golden stair!
And may all at last God's mercy know, when sinking
    on Earth's breast,
"Where the wicked cease from troubling and the
    weary are at rest."

FREDERICK GEORGE LEE.

All Saints', Lambeth,
    Nov. 1, 1877.

AURORA.

I.

UNFALL, and yet no night! Fire floods
    the earth!
   A molten rainbow flakes the northern
    sky!
The Polar gates unclose; and gleaming forth
   Troop the wild flames that glide and glare on high,
   Tinged in their vaulted home with that deep
    ruddy dye!

II.

Whence flash these mystic signals? what the scene
   Where the red rivers find their founts of flame?
Far, far away, where icy bulwarks lean

Along the deep, in seas without a name:
Where the vast porch of Hades rears its giant frame!

III.

The underworld of souls! sever'd in twain:
One, the fell North, perplexed and thick with gloom;
And one, the South, that calm and glad domain,
Where asphodel and lotus lightly bloom
'Neath God's own Starry Cross, the shield of peaceful doom.

IV.

No quest of man shall touch—no daring keel
Cleave the dark waters to their awful bourne:
None shall the living sepulchre reveal
Where separate souls must throng, and pause; and yearn
For their far dust, the signal, and their glad return.

v.

Ay! ever and anon the gates roll wide,
    When whole battalions yield their fudden breath;
And ghofts in armies gather as they glide,
    Still fierce and vengeful, from the field of death:
      Lo! lightnings lead their hofts, and meteors glare beneath.

ROBERT S. HAWKER.

Morwenftow,
November 10, 1870.

MY HOME.

MAY all good angels watch around my dwelling,
    May holy spirits shield it with their care,
Each wayward thought within its precincts quelling:
    I ask a blessing on it, in my prayer,
    From Thee, O Lord, Who rulest everywhere.

Angel of sleep, O may'st thou ever carry
    Unto its inmates visions fair and bright!
Angels of Peace and Love, within it tarry
    And shed around this hearth thy radiant light:
    Angel of Strength, defend it through the night.

Angel of Hope, when we are lone and dreary,
    Whisper that dawn will follow midnight shade;
Angel of Faith, when our sad hearts are weary,
    Uplift thy regal banner undismayed
    Before pale phantoms which make us afraid.

My Home.

Home, whence I truſt to paſs to life immortal
    When the calm ſleep of Death hath cloſed mine
        eyes;
I look upon thee only as the portal
    Of God's bright Manſion far beyond the ſkies—
    Of the reſplendent Home in Paradiſe!

                        HELEN MONTAGU STUART.

ALPHABETICAL LIST OF AUTHORS.

AKERS, George.
ALEXANDER, William.
BATT, Nora.
BAYNES, Robert Hall.
BLEW, William John.
C. A. M. W.
CASWALL, Edward.
CLYNE, Norval.
DE VERE, Aubrey.
DIX, William Chatterton.
DOLBEN, Digby Mackworth.
EARLE, John Charles.
GREEN, William Edward.
HAWKER, Robert Stephen.
LEE, Elvira Louisa.
LEE, Frederick George.
MONSELL, J. S. B.
MORGAN, Arthur Middlemore.

Moultrie, Gerard.
Mozley, H. W.
Newman, John Henry.
Oxenham, Henry Nutcombe.
Pierpoint, Folliott Sandford.
Purchas, John.
Ranking, B. Montgomerie.
Rossetti, Christina G.
Stuart, Helen Montagu.
"The Departed and other Poems," The Authoress of.
Vicars, Hedley.

INDEX OF FIRST LINES.

	PAGE
A HOUSE of prayer once confecrate	28
Another fleeting day is gone	120
As childhood wanes our dreams become lefs fair	72
A fad fweet end	35
A ftately Palace of the Triune God	18
A Temple, backed with trees and bafed with turf	91
At morn I plucked a rofe and gave it Thee	11
Babe, awake! the fun is high	31
Brother! after fet of day	37
Carol while yet thy life is in its fpring	151
Come, bleft Redeemer of the earth	147
Could fhe, that Deftined one, could fhe	118
Down below, the wild November whiftling	1
Gone, for them, the time of forrow, paffed for ever toil and pain	138
Hail, my guardian fpirit, hail	98
How long, O Saviour, wilt Thou ftay?	124
I made myfelf a myrtle crown	131
I make not fongs, but only find	107
In the ancient ftory	73
In the myftic realm of flumber, in the quiet land of reft	84

Index.

	PAGE
I saw "the waves of this troublesome world," raging and dark and cold	111
Is this, indeed, our ancient earth?	20
Let the sun summon all his beams to hold	6
Lord of the living and the dead	104
May all good angels watch around my dwelling	165
Musing over friends departed, loved ones known and missed and gone	159
Night falls apace, the shades grow long	41
O Eastward speed in gentle thought	94
O Lord, we know that all who love Thy Name	114
O to have wandered in the days that were	22
O toilers in Life's vineyard	155
Oh union wonderful and true	96
Praise, O praise the Lord of Heaven	108
Press each on each, sweet wings, and roof me in	76
Ruthlessly the bare bright wheel of antique Time goes round	13
Say not that hours are lonelier now and darker	126
She was his playmate when a child: and in Life's golden hours	44
Sunfall, and yet no night! Fire floods the earth!	162
The blasts of chill December sound	149
The Vesper Bell is pealing soft	115
The day was done: beside the sultry shore	54
The grass is rank, the shades are deep	141

Index.

	PAGE
The World is very foul and dark	59
The fun fhines bright and glorious, and the hill tops are illumed	62
Thy Hands have made me! in foul-faving flood .	66
'Twas feftal day in Heaven	79
We give Thee thanks, O Lord our God . . .	136
When man abode in Paradife	144
When by Thine altar, Lord, I kneel . . .	87
When tempefts ceafe at clofe of day	69
Whifper the angel voices foft and kind . . .	134
White is the colour of angels	56
White were the ftairs of marble ftone . . .	102
Why fhould we vex our foolifh minds . . .	122

CHISWICK PRESS:—C. WHITTINGHAM, TOOKS COURT, CHANCERY LANE.

www.ingramcontent.com/pod-product-compliance
Lightning Source LLC
Chambersburg PA
CBHW031444160426
43195CB00010BB/837